MY PUPPY'S FIRST
Journal

Photographs by Emily Rieman
Text by Michelle Goodman

SASQUATCH
BOOKS

My homecoming story

Where I came from

How my person knew I was "the one"

Radar

My first day with my new family

When I arrived at my new home, I immediately began to

Those first few hours, I spent a lot of time sniffing the

What I did that day to win over my new family

What my new family did to make me feel at home

Clara

My first night in my new home

I slept

○ **In a crate**
○ **On a dog bed**
○ **On the couch**
○ **In my person's bed**
○ **Other:** _____

In the middle of the night, I

In the morning, I

My first portrait

Paste photo here

My new pack

My two-legged family members

My four-legged family members

My favorite siblings

My rivals

Abby and Ozzie

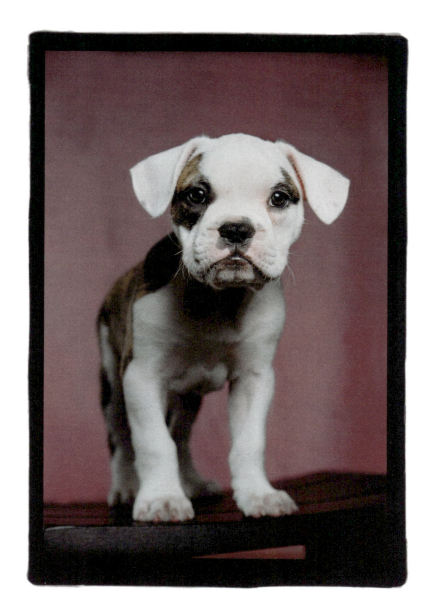

Tony

My role models

Who in my new pack I look like the most

Who I act like the most

What's in a name?

My full name

Whom or what I'm named after

My nickname(s)

How I earned these monikers

Lou

Otis

My dashing good looks

My breed (or unique blend thereof) is

My coloring is

My eyes are

My coat is

My tail is

My unique markings are

My winning personality

- ○   I'm the leader of the pack.
- ○   I'm happy to follow your lead.

I can best be described as

- ○   An adventure hound
- ○   A couch potato
- ○   A wallflower
- ○   Curious George
- ○   Dennis the Menace
- ○   Nervous Nelly
- ○   A diva who likes to be waited on hand and paw
- ○   Other: _____

_____

More about my personality

Hershey

My measurements

When I arrived at my new homestead, I

○ **Weighed this much:** _____

○ **And was this tall:** _____

After three months, I

○ **Weighed this much:** _____

○ **And was this tall:** _____

Six months down the line, I

○ **Weighed this much:** _____

○ **And was this tall:** _____

A year later, I

○ **Weighed this much:** _____

○ **And was this tall:** _____

Louie

My autograph

To capture paw prints, use a nontoxic ink pad (found at many toy, craft, and hobby shops). Remember to wipe paws clean when done.

Upon my homecoming

Three months old

Six months old

One year old

My medical history

What shots I've had and when

What shots I need and when

The family jewels

- ○ **Date I was fixed:** _____
- ○ **Date when I'm getting fixed:** _____
- ○ **No way am I getting fixed.**

Notes on my diet and health

A dog's home is his castle

Favorite nighttime sleeping spot

Favorite daytime sleeping spot

Favorite hiding spot

Favorite place to bury things

Favorite place to play

Favorite piece of furniture

Parsnip

Otis

The castle grounds

Outside, I have my own

- ○ **Patch of grass**
- ○ **Yard**
- ○ **Dog run**
- ○ **Dog house**
- ○ **Fire hydrant**
- ○ **Other:** _____

My daily routine

When I rise and shine each day

The first thing I like to do in the morning

What time I eat each day

When I like to nap

When playtime begins

What time I go to bed each night

Creature of habit

My person thinks it's adorable when I

My person thinks it's less than adorable when I

I always get in trouble when I

I get extra kisses and treats when I

Hershey

Zuri

Feeding time

I eat

- ○ **So quickly I forget to chew**
- ○ **Slowly, because I'm kind of fussy about food**
- ○ **Sporadically, throughout the day**
- ○ **Only when someone's looking**
- ○ **Only when no one's looking**
- ○ **Only when my four-legged family members come nosing around**
- ○ **Other:** _____

_____

_____

_____

After I eat, I like to

I like to nosh

Favorite puppy treats

Favorite people food

I'm a

- ○ **Drooler**
- ○ **Beggar**
- ○ **Thief**
- ○ **Other:** _____

_____

_____

My best story about stealing people food

Red

Finnegan

Playtime

- ◯ **I like it ruff.**
- ◯ **Please be gentle with me.**
- ◯ **Other:** _____

_____

_____

_____

My favorite toys

The games I could play 24/7

Duncan

Snuggle time

I'm a

- ○ **Leaner**
- ○ **Licker**
- ○ **Lapdog**
- ○ **None of the above; I like my space**
- ○ **Other:** _____

I live for

- ○ **Belly rubs**
- ○ **Butt scratches**
- ○ **Ear massages**
- ○ **Full body massages**
- ○ **Other:** _____

_____

_____

_____

What I do when I get any of the above

Penny

Sleepy time

Before I lie down I like to

- ○ **Fluff up my bed**
- ○ **Fluff up my person's bed**
- ○ **Fluff up my person's pillow**
- ○ **Fluff up the couch**
- ○ **Turn around in circles no less than three times**
- ○ **Other:** _____

_____

_____

_____

I like to snooze

- ○ **Sitting up**
- ○ **Snuggled with my favorite toy**
- ○ **With my head in my person's lap**
- ○ **On my back with all four legs in the air**
- ○ **Other:** _____

_____

_____

_____

Archie

Dexter

Dream a little dream

When I'm asleep

- ○ I hang my tongue out
- ○ My eyes flutter
- ○ My feet twitch as if I'm chasing rabbits
- ○ I whimper and wiffle
- ○ I snore like a drunken sailor
- ○ I always get blamed for any mystery smells in the room
- ○ Other: _____

_____

_____

What my owners think I dream about

What I really dream about

Gus

Going potty

When I started going outside

How my person got me to do this

How many accidents it took to get to this point

Worst accident I ever had

My ever-changing moods

I grin when

I pace when

I jump up on my hind legs when

I chase my tail when

I pout when

I hide behind my person's legs when

I act like a guard dog when

I slink off hoping no one will notice when

I'm most bored when

I get anxious when I see or hear (hats, planes, et cetera)

I bark my head off when

My trademark look

- ○ **Head tilted**
- ○ **Ears perked up**
- ○ **Head tilt/ear perk combo**
- ○ **Eyebrow furrow**
- ○ **Snaggletooth**
- ○ **Fur on my back raised**
- ○ **One-sided drool strand**
- ○ **Two-sided drool strand**
- ○ **Other:** _____

Winnie

Alistair

The world according to dog

Everyone knows my motto is

- ○ "Are you gonna eat that?"
- ○ "Is it time to play yet? **OK**, how about now?"
- ○ "Last one on the couch is a rotten egg!"
- ○ "Whatever it was, I didn't do it."
- ○ "The cat did it. I swear."
- ○ **Other:** _____
  _____
  _____

My best friends

Two-legged pals

My favorite things to do with them

Four-legged pals

My favorite things to do with them

The thing my person makes me do that I hate most

What I love most about my person

A few of my favorite things

Best dog park

Best pet supply store

Best thing to watch out the window or front door

Best item to chew that I'm allowed to chew

Best item to chew that I'm *not* allowed to chew

If I could be anywhere right now, I'd be

- ○ At the doggie parlor, getting a wash, cut, blow-dry, and pedicure
- ○ At the park, chasing dogs, tennis balls, or a Frisbee
- ○ In a lake, paddling after some dog, tennis ball, or Kong
- ○ On the couch
- ○ In my person's bed, with my head on their pillow
- ○ In the pantry, with my head submerged in a bag of dog food
- ○ Other: _____

_____

_____

My pet peeves

Number these items in order of the most hated

- ☐ Visiting the vet
- ☐ Getting my nails clipped
- ☐ Taking a bath
- ☐ Thunderstorms
- ☐ Fireworks
- ☐ The mail carrier
- ☐ The cat
- ☐ Other: _____

_____

_____

_____

_____

_____

Dash

Mary

Pup culture

Favorite books

Favorite magazines

Favorite songs

Mia, Tyke, Chenille, Diva, Gyro, and Tasha

More pup culture

Favorite TV shows

Favorite movies

Celebrity or public figure I most resemble

Kip

A first time for everything

The first time I went for a ride in the car, I

The first time I went to the vet, I

During my first bath, I

The first time I went to the park, I

The first time I went to puppy school, I

My first playdate was with

My first dogfight was with

My first catfight was with

The well-groomed canine

My bathing and grooming schedule

My collar looks like

I'm into/not into nail polish [circle one]

I'm into/not into bows [circle one]

I'm into/not into bandanas [circle one]

Tivon

Ruby

The dirt on bathing

What I really think of baths

What I do to let my person know my true feelings on the matter

Which one of us gets wetter from the experience

My post-bathing rituals

Once I'm squeaky clean, my person rewards me with

In turn, I like to reward my person by

- ○ Rolling in the dirt
- ○ Rolling in something worse
- ○ Rubbing my wet body on all the furniture in the house
- ○ Rolling in something worse and then rubbing my body on all the furniture in the house
- ○ Other: _____

_____

_____

Water, water everywhere

Regardless of how I feel about baths, I love

○ **Swimming in the lake**

○ **Trying to dunk myself in my water dish**

○ **Lying in my kiddie pool during summer**

○ **Rolling in mud puddles**

○ **Walking in the rain**

○ **None of the above; I don't like getting wet at all**

○ **Other:** _____

_____

_____

What's up, Doc?

How I react when I walk into the vet's waiting room

Worst scare that landed me at the vet

How much that visit cost my person

Rutledge

Pedal to the muzzle

When I hear the jingle of the car keys, I

○ Get so excited, I start dancing a jig

○ Run to my bed, curl up in a ball, and hope no one finds me

○ Remain as calm, cool, and collected as always

○ Other: _____

_____

_____

During car rides, I like to

○ Hang my head out the window

○ Pace and whine

○ Sleep soundly

○ Ride in the front

○ Ride in the back

○ Ride in my owner's lap

○ Bark at dogs walking by

○ Drool on my owner's shoulders

○ Throw up

○ Other: _____

_____

_____

Lily

What I did on my summer vacation

The coolest road trip we ever took was to

Where we stayed

What we did while we were there

The number of pictures my person took of me

Finnegan

More notes from my favorite vacation

My action shot

Paste photo here

Mia

Dog about town

When we go out, I get all gussied up in my

○ **Harness**
○ **Fleece jacket**
○ **Raincoat**
○ **Backpack**
○ **Pink studded collar**
○ **Other:** _____

_____

_____

My favorite place to go

My favorite person to go with

I know we're almost there when I can see or smell the

A walk in the park

When I'm on a walk, I like to

○ **Mark my territory**

○ **Scout out squirrels**

○ **Keep my nose to the ground and sniff everything in sight**

○ **Scavenge for "food" in the bushes**

○ **Other:** _____

_____

_____

_____

_____

_____

_____

The most exciting walk I've taken

Badger

The great outdoors

I'm a

○ **Digger**

○ **Hunter**

○ **Canine garbage can that eats anything off the ground**

○ **Other:** _____

_____

_____

My favorite place to dig

My favorite thing to chase

I once caught a

Unwelcome items or creatures I've brought into the house

The grossest thing I ever ate

My favorite thing to roll in

Sophie

Entertaining at home

When visitors come to the door, I immediately

When visitors make it into the living room I greet them by

- ○ Presenting my butt for them to scratch
- ○ Presenting my slobbery toy for them to throw
- ○ Licking their entire face
- ○ Placing my dirty paws on their immaculate white shirt
- ○ Sniffing their crotch
- ○ Eating their shoe
- ○ Mounting their shoe
- ○ Piddling on their shoe
- ○ Other: _____

_____

_____

The best time I ever had when guests came over

Fritz

Valiant

A canine and a scholar

According to my person, this is how smart I am:

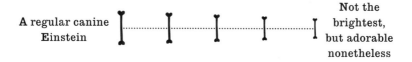

A regular canine Einstein   Not the brightest, but adorable nonetheless

According to my person's friends, this is how smart I am:

A regular canine Einstein   Not the brightest, but adorable nonetheless

According to yours truly, this is how smart I am:

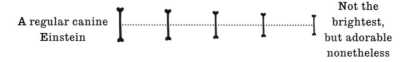

A regular canine Einstein   Not the brightest, but adorable nonetheless

Toby

Higher learning

Classes I'm taking

My teacher's name

I'm studying to be

○ **A good dog**
○ **A master Frisbee catcher**
○ **The canine Fred Astaire**
○ **State agility champion**
○ **An AKC winner**
○ **Other:** _____

_____

_____

What my teacher says about me

My vast knowledge

New tricks I've mastered

○ **Sit**   Date learned:

○ **Stay**   Date learned:

○ **Shake**   Date learned:

○ **Speak**   Date learned:

○ **Roll over**   Date learned:

○ **Other:**   Date learned:

○ **Other:**   Date learned:

New commands I've learned

○ **No jumping**   Date learned:

○ **No biting**   Date learned:

○ **No chewing**   Date learned:

○ **Other:**   Date learned:

○ **Other:**   Date learned:

Foustie

Coco

The most amazing trick
my person taught me

Luke

My impressive vocabulary

I bark when

I whine when

I snarl when

I howl when

Now you're talking

Words that make my ears perk up

Words that make me run and hide

The most unusual words I know

Mary

My flawless manners

What my person wishes I wouldn't do when they're not home

What my person wishes I wouldn't do when company's over

What my person wishes that the older dogs
I know didn't teach me to do

What my person tells me to never do when we're out in public

Annie

Confessions of a bad dog

The most valuable item I destroyed was

What my person did when they discovered the evidence

○ Happily for my person, I learned my lesson and never did that again.
○ I have yet to see the error of my ways.

The absolute most god-awful thing I ever did

Charlie

Louie with his mother and aunt

Working like a dog

If I could have any classic dog job, it would be

○ Herding sheep or cattle

○ Pulling a sled

○ Working as a service dog

○ Working as a police dog

○ Doing search and rescue

○ Hunting birds

○ Carrying a thermos of whiskey around my neck for my master

○ Lying in the lap of a fabulously wealthy heiress while getting a back massage

○ Other: _____

_____

_____

If I could have any classic human job, it would be

Gordon

My first birthday

Now that I'm growing up, I'm becoming more

- ○ Independent
- ○ Sneaky
- ○ Brave
- ○ Charming
- ○ Naughty
- ○ Well-behaved
- ○ Affectionate
- ○ Confident
- ○ Stubborn
- ○ Mellow
- ○ Other: _____

Zelda

Jasper

Reflections on my first year

What I love most about my new family

Guinness

What I do that makes my person's heart melt

Hank

Reasons I'm looking forward to my first year as an adult dog

My portrait at one year old

Paste photo here

Photographer **Emily Rieman** established her pet portrait business, Best Friend Photography, in 1997. She attended the School of Visual Arts (NYC) and the University of Washington, where she received a BFA in Photography. Her work has been published commercially and editorially. She lives in Seattle with her husband, Mark, and their dogs, Dexter and Stella.

Michelle Goodman is author of the *The Anti 9-to-5 Guide: Practical Career Advice for Women Who Think Outside the Cube* (Seal Press, 2007) and the popular blog, Anti9to5Guide.com. Her articles and essays have appeared in *The Bark, Bust, Bitch, CityDog, Salon, Canadian Living,* the *Seattle Times,* and several anthologies. She lives in Seattle with her 80-pound lap dog, Buddy.

Printed in China
Published by Sasquatch Books
Distributed by PGW
15 14 13 12 11 10 09 08 07   9 8 7 6 5 4 3 2 1

Cover and interior design: Kate Basart/Union Pageworks
Interior illustrations: Kate Basart/Union Pageworks

Library of Congress Cataloging-in-Publication Data is available.

ISBN-10: 1-57061-523-3
ISBN-13: 978-1-57061-523-8

Sasquatch Books
119 South Main Street, Suite 400
Seattle, WA 98104
(206) 467-4300
www.sasquatchbooks.com
custserv@sasquatchbooks.com

Ruby

This Journal Belongs to: _____

Emergency contact information

Veterinarian

_____

_____

_____

_____

24-hour emergency clinic

_____

_____

_____

Local pet shelter

_____

Pet license and microchip ID number

_____

_____

Microchip phone number to call if I'm lost

_____

Friends' and family's names and numbers

_____

_____

_____

_____

_____